TRAVELER'S GUIDE
TO
PERSONAL SECURITY

TRAVELER'S GUIDE
TO
PERSONAL SECURITY

SAM ROSENBERG

iUniverse, Inc.
Bloomington

TRAVELER'S GUIDE TO PERSONAL SECURITY

iUniverse books may be ordered through booksellers or by contacting:

iUniverse
1663 Liberty Drive
Bloomington, IN 47403
www.iuniverse.com
1-800-Authors (1-800-288-4677)

ISBN: 978-1-4759-4570-6 (sc)
ISBN: 978-1-4759-4571-3 (ebk)

Library of Congress Control Number: 2012915111

Printed in the United States of America

iUniverse rev. date: 08/25/2012

TABLE OF CONTENTS

I want to express my sincere thanks to my friend, mentor, and editor Rodger Morrow. You're the best!

Sam Rosenberg

FOREWORD

by Sam Rosenberg

Most of us can still remember a time when the most a traveler had to worry about was communicating with the cab driver or knowing when and whom to tip. Sadly, that age of innocence is long past.

The globalization of crime and terrorism didn't begin, of course, with 9/11, but there's no question that the risks and uncertainties of travel—and all areas of personal security—loom far larger in its wake. Not only are longer lines at airport security a fact of life for most travelers, but we also experience greater anxiety about the people we encounter and the situations in which we find ourselves.

The main goal of this guide is to replace this anxiety—much of which is likely unfounded—with a realistic understanding of what people and situations are (and are not) likely to pose a risk to your security and well being while traveling domestically or abroad. In its pages, you'll find most of the common situations in which you may be placed at risk and learn how to spot the warning signals of an impending attack or crime.

But even the most vigilant and knowledgeable people occasionally make mistakes or let their guard slip. So we also want to equip you with active countermeasures you can take to escape becoming a victim if you identify an attack already set in motion.

Our INPAX® philosophy is simple: *While it's good to have a lifeguard, it's better to know how to swim.* Personal security is a fundamental human need, and first and foremost, a *personal* responsibility—not something to be delegated to security professionals and police. We've found that most people can, with a minimal investment of time and effort, develop the understanding, the mindset and the skills to reduce dramatically their chances of becoming a victim.

Terrorism, kidnapping, and street crime are facts of life in many parts of the world. And while most Americans regard these as "Black Swan" events—rare, unpredictable and hence uncontrollable—the reality is quite different. They follow a logic that's all too predictable once it's properly understood. Being able to read and follow "predatory logic" is essential to avoiding becoming a target—and to extricating yourself from a situation once you have been targeted.

We hope the following pages will go a long way to making your travel, and your life, safer and more enjoyable.

Live with Confidence!

Sam Rosenberg

Chapter One

SECURITY LOGIC

"We don't rise to the level of our expectations, we fall to the level of our training."

—Archilocus, ca. 645 BCE

The first step to security—in any situation—is to cultivate the ability to identify, process and comprehend the critical elements of information that could alert you to a potential threat.

We refer to this knowledge as situational awareness.

Simply stated, it's *knowing what's going on around you.*

Fortunately, through many millennia of human evolution (as both predators and prey), we have all been equipped with this ability to varying degrees, though some of us may seem to be more in tune with our so-called "sixth sense" than others.

As a child, you may have been given picture puzzles and asked to identify "What's wrong with this picture?" As you scanned the image, you discovered some detail that was out of place—say, a man walking down the street in a hat and winter overcoat on a broiling summer day.

Recognizing incongruities

Child's play, you might say. True enough—but with a purpose. Our brains are hard-wired to scan our environment constantly for incongruities and to alert us to any possible danger they might represent. Gavin DeBecker calls this "the gift of fear," in his bestselling book of the same name.

The ability to recognize incongruities as we move through our environment, however, is much less a sixth sense—some mystical, almost psychic ability with which only a few are endowed—than a survival mechanism built into the limbic system of our brains that enables rapid (though largely unconscious) cognition in the face of a potential threat to our wellbeing.

Building on our "children's puzzle" example, imagine that you are standing in the teller line at your local bank branch on a warm July day when a someone walks in wearing a heavy, bulky coat. What would your "sixth sense" tell you? Would the hair on the back of your neck stand up?

Without consciously knowing it, you are already practicing *situational awareness*—the rapid cognition that occurs when something vaguely incongruous enters your field of view.

Unfortunately, most of us are so preoccupied with the cognitive chatter of our own lives ("Did I remember to fill out my deposit slip?" "Boy, this line is taking forever. Did I put enough money in the parking meter?") that we may not even notice the man in the overcoat.

And we find quickly ourselves on the floor with our hands over our heads while the man in the overcoat points a gun to our temple and tells us what to do.

Our innate situational awareness may have been there. We may recall, after we survive our ordeal, "Yes, I do remember the man in the overcoat walking in." But our preoccupation with other matters overrode our sixth sense, and we failed to take the proper course of action (leaving the bank immediately).

Victimology 101: the typical poor SAP

Let's break down what typically happens, physically and psychologically, when you're faced with a threat with which your experience and conditioning have not likely prepared you: Walking to your car in a parking garage when someone appears, seemingly out of nowhere, with a gun pointed directly at your face.

First, you're faced with a **stimulus**—the gun in your face. Your body's "startle" reflex is engaged and your brain (which was probably preoccupied with something else) shifts its focus to this new "information."

Immediately, you bring to bear all your knowledge and experience as you **analyze** what is happening. At the same time, your body is dumping adrenaline into your bloodstream like a tanker plane dropping water on a forest fire.

And then—as tends to occur when something happens to you that's completely outside your range of experience—you do one of two things: You **panic** and take flight (less likely), or you stand there **paralyzed** and quaking with fear (more likely).

We call this process SAP: Stimulus—Analysis—Paralysis (or Panic).

And that, in effect, is what you are: Some "poor sap" that people will hear about in tomorrow's news.

Beyond Paralysis: The Four Key Steps of SAFE

Fortunately, SAP isn't the inevitable outcome of an unexpected event like the one we've just described.

And that's where knowledge, experience and conditioning come into play. They enable us to avoid **paralysis** or **panic** and instead **formulate a plan** and **execute it successfully**.

We call this process SAFE:

> **S**—Size up the situation (stimulus)
> **A**—Analyze your options
> **F**—Formulate a plan
> **E**—Execute it and escape

Through study and training we can override our natural tendency toward paralysis or panic in a threatening situation—much as rock climbers condition themselves not to cling like a wet towel to the rock face but to lean out from it, in order to gain maximum mobility and a clear view of the available holds.

With sufficient practice and effort, nearly anyone can develop a capacity for what Hemingway described "grace under pressure"—the ability to keep the mind active and working in circumstances when it wants nothing more than to shut down.

Developing situational awareness—through training and experience—allows your brain to make the cognitive leap from SAP to SAFE.

The Continuum of Conflict

Some threats to your security are *objective* threats—a hotel fire, a natural disaster, a vehicle crash. Because the source of the threat is largely impersonal, the brain processes it differently than a threat from another human being. It is easier to maintain detachment and keep one's wits about one when dodging traffic in a busy intersection than when being menaced by someone with a gun—even though the risk of being killed may be comparable. Psychologists have even coined the term Complex Post-Traumatic Stress Disorder (CPTSD) to describe the more serious effects that trauma resulting from interpersonal conflict produces.

It's important to understand that human conflict exists on a continuum, and your objectives and priorities depend largely on what phase of this continuum you are addressing. Confrontations can, and generally do, progress along this continuum in a linear way—or may, in some rare circumstances, skip stages entirely (e.g., a surprise physical assault with no opportunity to avoid or negotiate).

Stage 1: Avoidance

Most people prefer and strive to avoid conflict whenever possible, and this natural ability to avoid conflict can be enhanced by developing one's innate situational awareness. Training can strengthen this natural avoidance ability, so that predators view you as a "hard" target and move on to another victim. This combination of awareness and training make you a difficult person to surprise and a target that predators will naturally tend to avoid.

Stage 2: Negotiation

It's been said that all human interaction takes the form of negotiation—a statement that implies both the inevitability of conflict and the need to manage it constantly. As will be discussed in Chapter 2 (Predatory Logic) most conflicts begin with some approach or "Interview" of the target. If avoidance fails (situational awareness), whether the situation escalates to something more dangerous or diffuses altogether is dependent on how you conduct that interview. Through training, it's possible in many situations to use and interpret verbal cues and body language (posturing) so that conflict remains at a low level and doesn't escalate into violence.

Stage 3: Response

When conflict cannot be avoided or negotiated, some level of physical action is required, whether successful or not. (If you manage to flee a conflict unharmed, or you hand over your purse without further conflict, the situation has been successfully negotiated.) Although self-defense training and techniques are beyond the scope of this handbook, we believe they play a critical role in successfully extricating oneself from any violent situation.

Understanding the continuum of conflict—from avoidance to negotiation to response—helps you better appreciate the thinking process that "bad guys" (be they street toughs or terrorists) apply to conflict when **you** are the target.

That "predatory logic" is the subject of the next chapter.

Chapter Two

PREDATORY LOGIC

I was a predator on the prowl for prey.

—Keith Eugene Wells
(convicted of clubbing two strangers to death
in the course of an armed robbery in Idaho)

Although predatory behavior is by no means confined to the human species, for the purposes of our discussion, we'll define a "bad actor"—or, more colloquially, "bad guy"—as a person who seeks to harm the safety or security of another.

Like conflict itself, "bad guys" exist on a continuum from the person who "loses it" after stressful day to the street criminals who cycle regularly through the criminal justice system to the professional terrorist who may have spent months or years honing his violent craft.

Although no hard-and-fast "bad guy" categories exist, it may be helpful to think of them as falling under three general headings we call the three "P's":

Potentials: These run the gamut from a "stressed-out" or mentally unbalanced individual (say, a disgruntled co-worker) to a temperamentally angry or aggressive person who, with the help of some alcohol or other intoxicant may become violent, often with seemingly slight provocation. All of us have some potential for violence, however slight, when we're angered, provoked or feel threatened. A "potential," in other words could be anyone, on "a bad hair day." This category can almost always be negotiated.

Predators: Essentially opportunistic criminals, predators exploit others—whether to enrich themselves, support a drug habit or simply to satisfy some primitive desire to dominate, injure or inspire fear. Most street criminals and con artists tend to fall into this broad group. If you are targeted by a Predator, how well you conduct the negotiation or "interview" will largely determine whether you will be viewed as a likely victim.

Professionals: We define professionals, not so much by *ability* (many are incompetent), but by *intent*. The professional bad guy can range from school and workplace shooters to terrorists or kidnappers. These criminals may be self-styled "idealists" who have a specific grudge or agenda, or may be attempting to execute a crime that requires a large degree of planning and organization to execute. While potential bad guys can almost always be deterred, a professional, once his plan has been set in motion, typically will not.

As one moves from Potential to Predator to Professional, however, the differentiating factor is the increasing level of

premeditation involved in executing the attack. A more carefully planned attack is necessarily more difficult to defuse or disrupt in its execution and may require greater training or experience to be able to spot.

That said, all bad guys (even non-violent ones) tend to employ a similar logic in the way they operate.

For the sake of memorability, however, we prefer to describe predator logic in terms of a familiar four-letter word T-I-M-E:

> **T**arget Selection
> **I**ntelligence (Interview)
> **M**ethod of Attack (Response dependent on type of attack)
> **E**scape/Exploitation (Ransom, terror claim of responsibility etc)

Let's look at them one at a time.

Target Selection

Depending on a predator's level of sophistication and proficiency, target selection may be simply a matter of spotting someone in an unguarded moment (talking or texting on a cell phone, using a urinal) and seizing the opportunity the situation presents. In other circumstances—generally involving a more complex class of criminal—it may involve many weeks or months of careful, methodical surveillance, understanding the target's daily routine and personal habits to create a "dossier" to aid in the development of the attack and to assist with subsequent escape and exploitation.

Recognizing all forms of target selection—from the opportunistic to the carefully planned and staged—is essential in developing situational awareness and avoiding becoming a target in the first place.

Intelligence (Interview)

Intelligence is the refinement of target selection into an action plan—where the raw data of initial surveillance is analyzed and processed. In a street crime, this is commonly described as the "interview" phase. Having made an initial selection of a potential target, the predator interacts with that individual ("Hey buddy, can you help me out here?") to determine whether they will escalate to an attack or simply move on to an easier victim. In more complex crimes such as kidnapping or terrorism, the intelligence phase may include numerous "dry runs," like those the 9/11 hijackers did in the weeks leading up to the attack.

In every case, it's vital to recognize when the intelligence phase is in progress, so as to be able to disrupt the predator's plans, "harden the target" and force him to move on to another victim.

Method of Attack

Law enforcement professionals speak of a criminal's mo., or *modus operandi,* the specific method that he uses to carry out a particular crime. This implies, however, that every attack by a given predator follows an identical form, unique and unmistakable, like the fingerprint left at a crime scene.

In reality, however, we are all constantly learning and evolving from our experience—even if we can't read a single word on a page. Predators use the knowledge they glean from previous attacks to hone their skills and make themselves less vulnerable to detection, resistance and capture. (In the case of bad guys for whom crime is a form of sexual release, the method may also change as the need for a greater "thrill" develops over time.)

Again, it is the knowledge and experience collected in the targeting and intelligence phases that determines the precise method of attack. So it's important to recognize that this method will likely evolve out of specific circumstances, designed to make the attack very difficult to resist. Although specific defensive tactics may be learned to minimize the success of an attack, recognizing predatory logic in its early stages is the best way to ensure the success of such tactics, when avoidance becomes impossible.

Bad guys are no less subject to paralysis or panic when their seemingly well-laid strategies seem to go awry. A situationally-aware "victim" can prove an unwelcome surprise, with the result being that the attack is abandoned and the predator himself has to worry about becoming the prey.

Escape/Exploitation

The phase immediately following the attack is most often what determines the predator's "success" or "failure"—both highly subjective and always gauged from the predator's point of view. With attacks where the focus is mainly on property, escape (with goods in hand) is the measure of success. Where the attack is primarily focused on the violence itself, escape may be less of a priority. (Some predators do harbor a pathological "need to be caught," though this is more common in film and television than in actual crime statistics.)

In terrorism and kidnapping, there is also often an exploitation phase, where demands are made or, in some instances, claims of responsibility. For victims, the exploitation phase may provide an opportunity for escape, as the predator shifts his attention away from the victim and toward a different point of focus.

Summing up

Situational awareness is critical to your safety in *any* situation, from crossing the street to surviving abduction. If you keep the mental model of SAFE in the back of your mind at all times (and thus avoid becoming a SAP), your chances of surviving a life-threatening confrontation are exponentially increased.

Remember, if avoidance fails and you find yourself in an "interview", how calmly and forcefully you negotiate it will generally determine whether the bad guy proceeds with his attack or moves on to easier prey.

Denial is pernicious, and will always attempt to seduce you into useless—and ultimately destructive—thought processes (e.g., "this can't be happening").

Aggressively refuse these thoughts.

Deny the opportunities as you can, deter when necessary, and be willing and able to defend should the need arise. Most of all accept situations for what they are and manage them to the best of your ability.

Ultimately knowing you can manage your environment, no matter what occurs regardless of the potential outcome, allows you to live not in fear or denial, but rather to live with confidence.

Chapter Three

IN THE OFFICE

In recent years, violence in the workplace has become a serious safety and health issue. Indeed, workplace homicide is now the fourth-leading cause of fatal occupational injury in the United States overall, and the number one cause of death in the workplace for women.

As a matter of corporate policy, most companies prohibit employees—as well as anyone else on company premises or engaged in a company-related activity (including customers and visitors)—from behaving in a violent or threatening manner, and frequently weapons are prohibited, except when carried by authorized security personnel. This is fine, however it rarely has a direct impact on whether or not violence in the workplace is going to occur—simply because a violent offender is not going to be deterred by a corporate policy. Not to mention the fact that many incidents of violence, which occur in workplaces, are in effect, domestic violence dynamics that have spilled over into the workplace, further demonstrating the impotence of corporate policies.

A more important paradigm to adopt is what we like to call a Commitment Based Security approach, in that every employee knows they are a vital and integral component of the security continuum as a whole.

One of the most profound commonalities of mass homicides in the workplace, and workplace violence in general, is the "telegraphing" of intentions long before an actual incident.

Disgruntled employees frequently talk about their intentions, threaten co-workers, or even make disturbing social media posts often long before an attack—similar to the way a person contemplating suicide may "cry for help" to those around them to intervene.

In incidents of domestic violence, managers may not be aware of boiling situations outside of the workplace with employees, but often peers or co-workers are aware of impending problems. This is not to suggest that everyone should be informing personal dynamics to management at every junction, but rather that it is everyone's job to use their intuitive faculties to know recognize when a situation outside the workplace may pose a threat to those inside the workplace and promptly notify the right people to take action.

There will always be those who read and interpret indicators *after* an incident and say "but I never thought he was serious . . ." The key to commitment based security is having everyone on the same team, educated how to understand what the pre-incident indicators of violence are, and committed to passing on vital information when concerned.

The intuitive faculties of all employees, working together, can virtually assure management that no piece of important data related to security slips through the cracks.

Any incident of violence—including threats of violence—should not be tolerated and must be immediately reported to management, human resources and security for action and investigation.

At INPAX®, we recommend that all employees—not just human resources managers and security personnel—be trained to recognize the warning signs of violence and to defuse potentially violent situations. Any discussion or meeting where emotions are likely to run high—for example, terminations or disciplinary meetings—should be considered for their potential to escalate into violence.

Here are some general guidelines to follow in situations where someone has issued a threat, begun to behave in a potentially violent manner or has already committed a violent and aggressive act:

- Consider the persons personal circumstances carefully when evaluating their potential for violence.
- Think of it as a spider web, with all of the strands of the web being elements of life which keep people grounded and rational—family, friends, work, children, extra-curricular activities, etc. The fewer the strands the greater the risk. If you appear to threaten the last remaining strand, violence may result, as the individual no longer perceives anything left worth living for.

- Other elements—substance abuse, access to weapons or a history of violence—are obvious factors to take into consideration.
- Corporate security or outside professional security intervention is always recommended in such cases.

If you have to negotiate with a potentially violent person

- Remember that **physical distance** between yourself and the individual is your **most important safety factor**. Your ability to react to a violent attack is diminished in direct proportion to your proximity to the attacker (or potential attacker). Once the attacker "closes the distance," your ability to respond or escape is sharply limited. Six feet between you and the individual is an *ideal* distance to maximize response time, with arm's length distance being an absolute minimum to respond or escape if he or she lunges at you.
- Any closer than arm's length and you must consider it *critical* distance, where your ability to physiologically respond is greatly compromised.
- A simple way to gauge ideal distance is if you can see his or her whole body, from feet to head peripherally, without having to move your head up or down, you are at an ideal distance.
- Interposing a barrier—a table or a desk—provides an additional measure of safety, but this should not be overestimated, as these can easily be lunged over or jumped by a highly emotional person.
- If the attacker has a weapon the need for physical distance is even greater. A blunt-force (e.g., a club or improvised club) or edged weapon can

easily double the ability of an attacker to cover the distance between you before you have time to react. To a violent person in the workplace, almost anything—from a chair to coffee mug to a potted plant—can become a weapon.

- By the same token, physical objects close to you can serve to shield you from the blows or strikes of a violent individual.

- Although self-defense techniques are beyond the scope of this handbook, it's helpful during the "negotiation" or "interview" phase of a confrontation (before an attack has been launched) to hold your hands up and in front of you with your palms open, in a "universal stop sign or simmer down, please" gesture. This allows you to deflect or intercept a blow should one be thrown, perhaps giving you a precious moment to re-establish distance and escape the situation.

- If possible, if someone has become violent (or shows the potential for imminent violence), you will want to isolate that individual in the building or area, both to protect other potential victims and to buy time to summon help.

- "Soft areas" of the workplace outside the zone where identification must be worn—such as parking lots or reception areas—are easier targets for workplace violence. Bear in mind that an estranged spouse, aggrieved ex-employee or street criminal may stage an attack in one of these areas, where security is generally more lax and where people are typically "in between" other activities (hence less likely to be aware of dangers or out-of-place individuals who may be lurking). See Chapter Seven ("In the Car") for more about parking lot security.

In the event of a workplace critical incident

- If you can escape, immediately flee the area, and get as far away from the work site as possible. Once safely away, call for help.
- If you cannot run, attempt to barricade yourself in an office or room, and call for help via cell phone or office phone if available.
- If you cannot run or hide, you must consider fighting back as a last resort. Use whatever improvised weapons may be available and always remember that "Courage is as contagious as fear"

Mail and Parcel Bombs

Law enforcement officials are warning of the possible increase in mail and parcel bombs. You should not open any unexpected packages and should follow company security protocols regarding any suspicious parcels, which may require you to contact local police and postal authorities.

Be suspicious of the letter or parcel if:

- The letter is uneven, lopsided, rigid or bulker than normal; there is evidence of discoloration, oil stains, or the material has an uncommon feel to it.
- The sender is unknown. There is no return address, and there are restricted comments on the parcel or letter such as "for your eyes only"

- The letter is "cut and paste" and labels are "homemade"
- The package or letter emits a peculiar odor, particularly the smell of almonds.
- There is excessive tape, or protruding wires, string or tinfoil.
- See Appendix A for US Postal Service Guide to Suspicious Parcels

Chapter Four

AT HOME

Although home security itself is not the focus of this handbook, it's still important to remember that your workday typically begins when you leave your house or apartment in the morning and only ends when you return at the end of the day. When you are working away from home—whether from a hotel or living in a house or apartment in a foreign country—the same routines and rhythms tend to manifest themselves in your behavior.

Simply stated, we're creatures of habit.

Bad guys—especially professionals—understand the workday routine of their victims all too well. During the target selection phase, they may carefully note the times you leave for work each morning and return each evening. What time do the lights come on and go off? What do you carry with you when you leave and come home? Do you stop anywhere along the way? Do you like to go out for lunch or stay in?

All these routines form the basis of the bad guys' "surveillance"—which can often be hard to detect, especially when conducted by a highly seasoned criminal.

Your best protection—beyond the simple situational awareness we covered in Chapter One—is to **vary your routine**. Unpredictable people make harder targets than people whose routines are so well established you can set your watch by them.

Varying the route of your daily commute, changing up your eating routine, running your errands in a different order (or, if possible, in different places) make the professional bad guy's job more difficult—and may encourage him to move on to an easier target.

GPS navigation systems make it easy to vary routes and waypoints, even in an unfamiliar city, and many of the latest smartphones now include GPS capability. Take advantage of this technology to make yourself harder to track—and hence to trap.

In high-risk situations abroad, you may want to add steps to your "routine" that have no purpose other than to confuse those who may be following you—(Refer to Chapter 6 on Street Wisdom for tactics you can follow if you think you are being followed.)

Forewarned is forearmed

Exercise a great deal of caution and suspicion around strangers or people taking an unusual interest in you or your family. You should not hesitate to utilize resources like sex offender locator sites, and one of the most valuable personal resources a family should have is a company that can provide professional, comprehensive background checks and vetting services.

All caregivers, and workers who would be inside or around your home or family, teachers, and daycare centers—even neighbors who raise suspicion, should be vetted.

Family Security Awareness

The vast majority of kidnappings, and child abductions occur within 3 blocks of the victims home, most within the immediate area around the home.

Not vetting those people allowed near your family exposes you and them to the worst kind of predators:

This happened in the case of 14-year-old Elizabeth Smart, who was abducted from her bedroom in Utah by Brian Mitchell, who had been employed at her home to do roofing work.

In the Smart case, the victim's father hired an unemployed drifter to do roofing work on the house, placing him in close proximity to his daughter. Ed Smart's failure to vet Brian Mitchell—something that could have been done with a couple of phone calls—nearly destroyed his daughter's life.

Chapter Five
AT THE HOTEL

When you travel—whether it's simply to an unfamiliar city or somewhere halfway around the world—you necessarily cede some of your "home field advantage" to the bad guys. You may be in a different time zone, coping with jet lag. You may find it more difficult to get from place to place. You may not speak the language or fully understand the local customs.

It's natural, then, that your hotel becomes your "home away from home"—typically staffed with friendly, helpful people who speak your language and depend for their livelihoods on making your stay feel safe and pleasant.

However, it's critical you always remember that you are *not* at home. For that reason, there are things you'll want to keep in mind when staying at hotels, using the services they offer and visiting the other local attractions (shops, restaurants, etc.) that your hotel concierge may point you to.

General Considerations

- At your hotel, request a room between the second floor and the ninth. (In less-developed countries, try to stay between the second and fifth floors.) This will make window entry difficult, but escape in the event of a fire possible with emergency equipment. If you are obliged to take a room on the first floor, keep the windows locked at all times.
- Insist that all the locks on your door work properly. If they do not, request a room change immediately. You may want to make a practice of carrying a simple door wedge (with or without an alarm) and get in the habit of using it in addition.
- Include a small flashlight and a smoke hood as part of your standard travel kit for use during a fire in a hotel or an electrical blackout.
- Under no circumstance should you open any package or envelope sent to your hotel without knowing the sender.

Soft Areas

- Keep your situational awareness "on high" when passing through the unsecured or "soft" areas of any hotel: lobbies, garages, restaurants and bars—especially while checking in.
- Terrorists most commonly launch attacks or detonate bombs from these soft areas, and they make fertile hunting ground for other predators looking for potential prey.

- If you are targeted for kidnapping (more in Chapter 10), one of the most reliable places for surveillants to acquire you as a target is arriving and particularly departing your hotel.
- Keep alert for "watchers" who might be taking an interest in you.
- By simply getting in the habit of practicing situational awareness on check-in, and any time traversing through the soft areas of the hotel, you make yourself a much harder target.

Getting to and Arriving at the Hotel

- If the country of your destination has a significant kidnapping problem, you should not be met at the airport by a high profile, high-risk resident associate in a company car.
- If you are to be met by a company driver or a junior staff member, you should know his or her identity before getting into the car. The driver under no circumstances should carry a sign with your name or your company's name on it. Coded signs are the preferred means for establishing contact.
- If you are traveling by taxi (see Chapter 9) to your hotel, select a franchised cab, as opposed to an independent or a gypsy cab. If you have misgivings about a particular taxi, turn it down.
- Avoid letting anyone know what your room number is, and ask front desk people to write the number down for you rather than verbalize it.
- When you first arrive and each time you come back to your room, check the closets and bathroom to

ensure that the room is secure before letting your guard down.

Food and Amenities

- Hotel restaurants are, almost invariably, the safest place to eat anytime you're in an unfamiliar or particularly hostile country.
- Simply avoiding unnecessary travel outside of the hotel, limits your exposure to street crime or predatory surveillance.
- Your room will most likely be entered in your absence, by cleaning staff and possibly others. Be aware that room safes in many parts of the world are not secure. Use the main hotel safe via the front desk to store valuables, IDs, passports, visas, etc. Don't leave anything in your room you don't want others to see (or possibly steal).
- In some countries, such as China, hotels are used to gather intelligence on guests. Using Internet services at a hotel can make your computer vulnerable. You should assume telephone conversations on hotel lines are tapped and rooms are bugged for sound—and probably video. Never leave a laptop, PDA or important documents in the room when away because the devices could be stolen, cloned or copied (more on Information Security in Chapter 9).

Hotels in High Risk Countries

Choose your hotel location carefully—ideally within a well-protected, walled compound and make sure your room is situated well away from the street. The hotel should have armed security and strong physical barriers to guard against intrusion.

A well-fortified hotel should have hydraulic wedges that enable hotel security to thoroughly examine each vehicle that enters the hotel perimeter. The approach to the hotel should have stout zigzag barriers to prevent a high-speed car attack.

In areas where fortified hotels aren't available, it may be possible to find a smaller hotel most likely not on terrorists' radar.

Alternatively, look for a low-rise hotel with multiple outbuildings and request a room as far from the lobby as possible. This will minimize your vulnerability to a suicide bomb attack.

In hotels that lack a fortified perimeter, be sure to request a room on one of the higher floors, even if you have to choose one above the 9th floor. Again, the room should not face the street and be well away from the main entrance.

Avoid hotels with underground parking garages, as they offer an easy target for car bombers.

In high-risk countries, it is wise to steer clear of places, other than hotels, in which Westerners congregate, including:

- Bars
- Restaurants
- Clubs
- High-end shopping centers
- Tourist attractions
- Christian and Jewish places of worship.

Outside the Hotel

- Restaurants and sidewalk cafes are common sites for a variety of crimes, including pick-pocketing, drugging and robbery.
- In countries where drugging is common—such as Turkey, Brazil, Colombia, Thailand and the Philippines—try to keep an eye on your food and drink at all times. When ordering drinks, ask for bottles or cans to be unopened or be sure to watch them being poured.
- When planning business meetings, make sure you have addresses and directions ahead of time. If you're going by taxi, ask the hotel or restaurant to call one for you.
- If you're visiting a location outside the city, apprise yourself of the perils before you depart. Most U.S. embassies have a regional security officer who can provide you with information.

- Always have the police emergency number and that of your embassy or consulate with you.
- Be particularly observant as you depart your hotel, and attempt to vary the times and exits that you use to make it more difficult to observe your comings and goings.

Chapter Six

STREET WISDOM

It's a game for two, and I get there first.

—Bank robber Clyde Barrow

Situational awareness depends on being knowledgeable about the environments you may find yourself in. Foreign travel poses a particular challenge in this regard, since local law and custom vary widely from country to country—and may be very different from those that prevail in the U.S.

Although we can't provide you with a detailed briefing on every situation you may encounter, we do offer some general guidelines on how to be "streetwise" wherever you go.

Bear in mind when reading this chapter that while many people go out of their way to treat everyone—irrespective of gender, skin color, nationality or religion—with the same level of decency and respect, bad guys seldom operate by the same rules of fair-mindedness. The same tolerance most of us take for granted in the workplace simply doesn't hold on the street and in certain parts of the world.

If, therefore, some of the following material strikes you as "politically incorrect," remember that we are describing the world, not as we wish it to be, but as it is. Our overriding goal is to keep you safe and secure.

Before you Travel

- Ensure that a personal profile package is on file with your company, friend or spouse and is kept up to date. The package should contain the following basic descriptive data on each traveler:
    - o Color photograph
    - o Height, weight, color of eyes and hair, scars/marks
    - o Handwriting samples
    - o Fingerprints
    - o Voice samples
    - o A description of any medical problems
    - o "Proof of life" questions. (Questions to which only your spouse or close colleagues know the answer) These questions would be for the use of law enforcement personnel during any negotiations if any executive or family member were to be taken hostage by criminal or terrorist kidnappers. A sample questions would be "What is the nickname of the victim's aunt who lives in upstate New York?"
- Anytime you travel outside the US, consider registering your trip with the US Department of State's S.T.E.P. Program (Smart Traveler Enrollment Program). STEP is designed to provide you with

critical and timely intelligence on in-country activities that could pose a security risk to American travelers and enables State Department personnel to more rapidly intervene should a problem occur.

- Additionally, once in-country, consider contacting the local US Consulate, and signing up to receive "Warden" notifications. The Warden Notification System is a method for reaching U.S. citizens and nationals in foreign countries in the event of emergencies, disasters or threats, and are provided by Department of State personnel stationed in country who often have the most timely local data.

- Make sure you make two photocopies of the identification page of your passport, your driver's license, and your credit cards. Leave one set of copies with family or friends back home, and take one with you.

- Consider exchanging your passport if it shows prior travel to countries whose policies are or were the subject of controversy, (e.g., South Africa or Israel). Incidentally, the US State Department will charge you for a new one. When you receive your new passport, go to a stationary store and purchase a plain cover for it.

- If you can, memorize your passport number, date and city of issuance.

- In some countries, such as Mexico, where law enforcement officials are often corrupt and may attempt to steal your passport if you are stopped for questioning, it is often advisable to leave your actual passport locked in the hotel safe (not the one in your room), and carry your photocopy with you instead.

- Consider traveling with a portable smoke hood and pocket flashlight. Both could mean the difference in escaping an airline accident or hotel fire, and the flashlight can further serve as an improvised self-defense tool.
- Travel as light as possible. Try not to travel with any unnecessary or valuable items, and never travel with anything you couldn't part with.
- If you travel with medications, ensure they are in the original package, and keep a copy of the prescription with you.
- Don't use luggage tags that display the your company's logo, country club membership, or other easily identifiable badges of wealth or exclusivity.
- Consider traveling with a "go-bag" (see Chapter 10 for details).

In Countries with Moderate Crime

- Your passport is your lifeline. Allowing it to fall into the hands of thieves or pickpockets could easily ruin your entire trip. Leave it in the hotel safe and carry your photocopy instead.
- If you must drink, do so only in the safety of your hotel or in establishments recommended by people you trust. Drugging by thieves or kidnappers is increasingly common in many parts of the world.

Travel to Muslim Countries

- The laws and customs of Muslim countries vary widely, and you should be well acquainted with these before setting out on your trip. Your local contacts can help in this regard.
- Among the items to be avoided are: alcoholic beverages of any kind; racy magazines, books, or videos; and material that may be regarded as offensive to Islam.
- As a rule, alcohol consumption should be avoided in Muslim countries, even when it may be offered.
- All travelers to Muslim countries should dress conservatively, especially women. Headscarves and black cloaks are necessary attire for women in many parts of the Muslim world. Slacks and outfits that bare any skin below the neck should be avoided
- Men should avoid socializing with Muslim women—and vice versa. In Saudi Arabia, men and women who venture in public together must be prepared to furnish proof of marriage.
- Photography should be avoided. In many countries it is considered offensive, in others, illegal.

Hostile Countries

- Don't bring cameras or any electronic equipment that might be considered "spy gear"
- If you bring a laptop, don't expect privacy or security of your data. In some countries, you may

be required to furnish passwords and access codes to the authorities. (See Chapter 9).

- Be aware of currency restrictions and convert dollars only in legally sanctioned exchanges. Use credit cards whenever possible.

- Don't travel with expensive jewelry, designer clothing or items that could be traded on the black market. These items could be subject to confiscation. They could also be used as evidence of your intent to engage in black market activities.

- Read your visa documents carefully and observe any restrictions they may place on your travel or activities.

- Don't engage in any activity that could be construed as "information gathering" about the host country.

- Avoid political discussions and controversial topics.

- Be forthright in your dealings with local authorities. False statements are very likely to land you in hot water.

- Avoid rental cars. Penalties for even the smallest traffic infractions can be very severe.

- If you purchase antiques, make certain that the seller furnishes you with a valid certificate of export.

- Never agree to carry anything out of the country for a local, no matter how innocent the request may seem.

- Stay in the country only as long as your business requires. Unnecessary touring and sightseeing only increase your exposure to risk.

Countries With Severe Terrorism or Crime

- Again, forewarned is forearmed. Try to learn as much as possible about recent terrorist or criminal activity in the areas you will be visiting.
- Airline reservations should be made in your own name, with no indication of your corporate affiliation.
- Keep your travel itinerary on a strictly "need to know" basis with colleagues, friends and family. Never share it with anyone you don't know well.
- Your itinerary should be provided to a corporate security representative. It should include travel dates, flight numbers, arrangements for ground transportation and local points of contact. Advise your security representative of any changes in plans.
- Carry only items essential for your trip. Expensive items will make you a target for criminals.
- Dress casually while traveling and as much as your in-country activities will permit. It is better to look like a tourist than an executive; tourists are less likely to be targeted for terrorism or kidnapping.
- Be cautious in talking to strangers while in transit, particularly when it comes to revealing your itinerary, the purpose of your trip or details about your job and family.
- When you fill out your landing card prior to arrival, provide only the minimum necessary information. Don't provide your job title or company affiliation under "occupation." Use only the generic term "businessperson." Be vague about your hotel

arrangements unless specifically asked by an immigration official.

Travel Tips for Women

- Avoid attire that might be considered provocative, especially in developing countries.
- If you can arrange a driver in advance through your hotel or local contacts, do so. If you must use a cab, make sure it is licensed, radio equipped and comes from the regular taxi line. Gypsy cabs are common in many countries—and an invitation to trouble.
- If the driver tries to place your luggage in the back seat, insist that he place it in the trunk. Refuse to sit in the front seat for any reason, and don't allow him to pick up any additional passengers. Don't be afraid to make a scene if you have to.
- If you must travel by yourself in a high-crime country, confine your meals to your hotel.
- Avoid walking on the street after dark.

Travel tips for nonwhites

- Persons of color may encounter security problems abroad, particularly in certain parts of Western Europe and the former Eastern bloc.
- "Skinhead" gangs in Germany and elsewhere have been known to target nonwhites and U.S. servicemen and women.

- To minimize these risks, it is best to restrict your activities to business centers and to wear conservative business attire while on the street.

If You Suspect You Are Being Followed

INPAX rarely advises confronting a surveillant directly.

Instead, if you think you are being followed, you should take steps to verify your suspicions.

To do so, you'll need to run what we call a simple Surveillance Detection Route, or SDR. From a practical standpoint there are only two times in which you might be both vulnerable to being followed and able to execute a simple SDR: while on foot and while driving a car.

1. *SDR while on foot:* The easiest way to ID a single surveillant while on foot is to use what we call the "zig-zag" method. Simply cross the street. If the surveillant crosses behind you, cross the street back again, if he or she follows you back to the original side, you have a good idea that something is amiss. If you want to be sure, you can either cross the street yet again, or run the "Crazy Ivan" SDR explained below, on foot.

2. *SDR while driving a car:* The simplest way to determine if someone is following you in a car, is to make four consecutive right hand turns, effectively traveling in a circle. If someone maintains pursuit through this process, it's a fairly good indicator that the car is following you. We call this SDR "Crazy

Ivan", affectionately named after the Russian submarine maneuver from the movie *The Hunt for Red October.*

Always remember that mobile surveillance is one of the most difficult processes to pull off effectively, especially against a target that has a fair level of situational awareness.

Typically only government intelligence services have the requisite manpower, training, resources, and equipment to pull it off properly without being detected, and often require numerous well-trained operatives and considerable resources.

Criminal and terrorists groups generally don't have the manpower, training and equipment to conduct surveillance properly.

If you are confident that you are being followed, you may choose to make it difficult for pursuit to continue.

Reverse Funneling: The concept of "reverse funneling" is simple: You enter an area with a central entrance, but numerous potential exits. For example, you may nonchalantly enter hotel lobby, head up an elevator, traverse a floor, return down the stairwell and out a side or rear exit. This procedure is nearly impossible to defeat, since it's impossible to cover all exits without enormous manpower and a great deal of skill in execution.

If you determine that someone (or a group) is following you, raise your alert level and immediately perform SDRs and reverse funneling as needed until you have the ability to notify either your company's security or local law enforcement if appropriate, and exercise a greater degree of caution in everything you do until your travel ends.

Bear in mind, if you are being watched by a government's intelligence service, you most likely will not know about it. However, in the event you do identify surveillance teams and feel they are government sanctioned, you may have to accept the dynamic that you will be followed and observed for the duration of your trip. This type of surveillance is rare, but not unheard of in some parts of the world.

All the more reason, why direct confrontations with surveillants should be avoided if at all possible.

Remember—situational awareness is your greatest ally, and forewarned is forearmed. Use good judgment when traveling, and if you think you are being followed, you may very well be.

Chapter Seven
TRAVELING BY LAND

Situational awareness tends to increase in proportion to our unfamiliarity with our environment. When we walk down a dark street at night, for example, we are more alert to potential danger signals than when we stroll down the driveway each morning to pick up the newspaper.

Since travel by car, bus or rail is more familiar to us than airline travel—and uniformed security personnel aren't usually around to remind us—we may let our guard slip when we get behind the wheel of a car or board a train. Statistically, we know we're more likely to be targeted as the victim of a crime, but familiarity overcomes reason, and we let the bad guy gain the tactical advantage of surprise.

This chapter is designed to help you become more aware of the risks that loom every time you operate or board a vehicle.

Taxis

Most travelers require the use of taxis to get around at some point during international travel. As a general rule, only take taxis clearly identified with official markings. Taxis available via taxi stands at airports and hotels are generally safe, but always beware of unmarked "gypsy" cabs.

You must know and remember that taxi drivers, in many countries such as Mexico and eastern Europe, sell intelligence on foreign visitors to criminal organizations, or may even be directly involved in kidnapping, robberies or worse. Always remain highly alert when traveling by cab, and only provide information on a need to know basis.

It is quite common for taxi drivers to engage travelers in conversations while in transit. Always assume that these conversations are for the purpose of intelligence gathering, and as such, treat them with extreme caution and suspicion. Common questions include:

- Where are you from?
- Are you here on business?
- What do you do?
- Are you here by yourself?
- How long are you staying?

It's best to avoid such conversations, but should you choose to engage them, be prepared to use some "white lies" to avoid indicating vulnerability. Here are a few examples of secure ways to answer common questions:

Q: *Where are you from?*

A: Canada. (In strongly anti-American countries or regions it's often best to avoid the subject altogether)

Q: *Are you here on business?*

A: No, I'm visiting friends. (This accomplishes two things, it reduces your potential value as a target as tourists are generally less desirable than business travelers, and it indicates that you have local contacts and are not here by yourself)

Q: *Are you here by yourself?*

A: No, I'm visiting friends (or) my wife/husband is at the hotel. (You want him to know that you will be missed locally if something should happen to you)

Q: *What do you do?*

A: I'm a schoolteacher, or receptionist, or nurse. (Obviously you want to downplay your true status if your position or occupation might skyline you as a wealthy target)

Q: *How long are you staying?*

A: I'm leaving tomorrow (or later today). (This greatly reduces your desirability as a target, as it doesn't allow time for a properly planned attack)

Please note, while it's a good idea to lie when necessary to taxi drivers or other suspect individuals, be very careful lying to an authority figure such as a law enforcement officer, even if you suspect he/she may be corrupt. Also, bear in mind that a good lie is always based at least partially on the truth. Don't invent a story that is so far removed from reality that you end up contradicting yourself, losing your confidence, or saying something obviously incorrect—this could actually increase your vulnerability.

Car Trouble

In many places frequented by Americans (e.g., southern Europe) victimization of motorists and travelers via busses and trains, has become commonplace.

- If you must rent a car when traveling, choose one that won't stand out in local traffic.
- If possible, choose a car with power door locks and power windows. These features give the driver better control of access.
- An air-conditioned vehicle also provides greater security, allowing you to drive with windows closed.
- If possible, don't park your car on the street overnight. If a parking garage is unavailable, select a well-lit area.
- Never pick up anyone not well known to you.
- Don't get out of the car if there are suspicious looking individuals nearby. Drive away.
- Be suspicious of anyone who hails you or tries to get your attention when you are in or near your car.
- Criminals may pose as good Samaritans, offering help for tires that they claim are flat or that they have made flat. Or they may flag down a motorist, ask for assistance, and then steal the rescuer's

luggage or car. Usually they work in groups, one person carrying on the pretense while the others rob you.

- Other criminals get your attention with abuse, either trying to drive you off the road, or causing an "accident" by rear-ending you.

Safety on Public Transportation

Criminal activity against public transportation varies widely from country to country. One of the best available sources on this kind of crime is the U.S. State Department website (http://travel.state.gov/travel/cis_pa_tw/cis/cis_4965. html).

Here are some general tips, however, for using public transportation:

Buses

- The same type of criminal activity found on trains can be found on public buses on popular tourist routes. For example, tourists have been drugged and robbed while sleeping on buses or in bus stations.
- In some countries, entire busloads of passengers have been held up and robbed by gangs of bandits.

Trains

- Robbery of passengers on trains along popular tourist routes are a growing problem, especially on overnight trains.

- If you find your way being blocked by a stranger, move away or you may find yourself blocked in. This can happen in the corridor of the train or on the platform or station.
- Don't be afraid to alert authorities if you feel threatened in any way. Police are often assigned to ride trains on routes where crime is a serious problem.
- If you're traveling overnight, book the entire sleeping compartment and don't permit other passengers to enter.
- Board the train with enough food and water for the journey. Don't purchase snacks or drinks from vendors on board—these could be drugged.
- Treat "new acquaintances" with suspicion, and decline any offers of food or drink.

Chapter Eight

TRAVELING BY AIR

Airline security has become much more stringent since the 9/11 attacks. Nevertheless, these improved security measures are being constantly monitored and tested by terrorist organizations, so it's important that you play an active role in safeguarding your own security—and above all maintain the situational awareness we discuss in Chapter One.

At the Airport

- Since 9/11, terrorist attacks have begun to focus on the so-called "soft areas" of the airport (and other public buildings generally) where security is less stringent.
- Keep your time in ticketing, ground transportation and public lobby areas to a minimum. These carry the highest risks of bombings and other terrorist incidents. Proceed as soon as possible to the security checkpoint and into the "sterile area" of the departure gates.

Aboard the Plane

- Eighty percent of all airline accidents happen during takeoff and landing. A tight and secure seat belt is your best defense.
- Count the number of seats between you and the closest exit, since smoke or darkness could impair your vision in an emergency.
- Consider traveling with a flashlight and smoke hood (see Appendix 2 on your "go-bag"), and have them readily available.
- Keep your cell phone in your pocket or "go-bag" should you have to make an emergency exit.
- In a crash, what you do in the first 90 seconds after the plane comes to a stop may decide your fate. Here again, situational awareness is essential.
- Don't release your seatbelt until the plane has come to a full stop and your have your bearings. Know where you are and where you want to exit before you make your move.
- If you have to evacuate in a hurry, leave your carry-on luggage, and get out. Anticipate considerable obstruction from baggage (and possibly bodies). Remember that speed is essential.

Hijacking

- The most important decision you will make in any hijacking or kidnapping situation is when to resist and when to comply. Remember that not all hijackers are suicidal, some may be seeking to make a political statement or to seek asylum in another country.

- In the early stage of an incident, you should be alert for any sign that death rather than money or ransom demands is the aim of the attack. You should also be aware that your captors may go to considerable lengths to conceal their motives.
- If it is clear that death and destruction is the aim, you have little choice but to resist by any means possible.
- Once a plane is in flight, hijackers often seize documents on a passenger's person or in his or her carry-on baggage. Potentially provocative items—including information that identifies you as a corporate executive—should be dispensed with or, if essential to the purpose of the trip, relegated to checked luggage.

Non-suicidal hijackings

- Try not to make eye contact with the hijackers, especially during the first 20 to 30 minutes, when the perpetrators are most anxious and agitated.
- If the hijackers demand valuables, documents or other personal items, comply without emotion. This is generally a sign that the attack is non-suicidal.
- Don't ask permission to do anything unless absolutely necessary.
- Don't talk with other passengers around you or do anything to lead your captors to think you're plotting against them . . .

- Keep calm and conserve your strength. Don't sleep unless absolutely necessary and only for brief periods.
- Accept any food, beverage or other "hospitality" offered by the hijackers.
- Prepare yourself to be interrogated by the hijackers, remembering that your personal effects could draw attention to you. Be as truthful as possible, but don't "blurt out the truth" if doing so would endanger your safety.
- Don't venture comments for or against the hijackers' cause. Play dumb and listen attentively.
- Use your time to analyze the situation and plan your actions in the event the situation deteriorates into violence.
- At the sound of gunfire or other disturbance, crouch as low as possible and remain in that position until you have no doubt that it is safe to sit back up or that you must take other action for your safety.
- In a non-suicidal hijacking, your best hope is for a negotiated release. That said, you have nothing to gain by remaining captive unnecessarily if you have an opportunity to escape. Once you have made that decision, however, don't second-guess yourself. Keep moving.

Suicidal hijacking

- If you conclude that the hijackers are suicidal, allow time for any sky marshals aboard the flight to take action. If such action isn't forthcoming, your best chance lies in joining other passengers in overpowering the hijackers, using whatever improvised weaponry may be at hand, including rolled-up magazines, pens or flashlights.

- Carry-on bags, briefcases, pillows and seat cushions may be used effectively as shields against edged weapons.

Chapter Nine

INFORMATION SECURITY

In a knowledge-based economy, information security has become almost as critical as personal security.

If sensitive company information falls into the wrong hands it could be extremely damaging to your business, and a loss or confidential personal information can place you at great risk of identity theft, kidnapping or worse.

Protecting Sensitive Information:

Many international companies—and so-called "friendly" foreign countries—engage in espionage. Some have even been known to use their national intelligence services to spy on visiting executives, especially if the executives' competition is state-subsidized. This has been known to occur in Russia, India and China, as well as in countries that many would not consider hostile in this area, such as France and Israel.

Often, hotels are used to gather intelligence on guests. Using Internet services at a hotel can make your computer vulnerable, and you should assume telephone conversations on hotel lines are tapped. Rooms may even be bugged for sound—and possibly video.

Further, there may be times where you are required by government or law enforcement officials to surrender access to computers and electronic devices for examination or confiscation.

Given these realities, consider the following guidelines to protect your data from being seized or compromised:

- Bring with you only information essential to the success of your trip.
- If you must bring along a computer, try to take a "clean" laptop—one that has no files or documents stored on it, or only those files necessary for the trip.
- Consider booting from a CD/DVD-ROM, which gives you a pristine operating system every time you boot. This precludes the use of keyloggers and other spyware that can be surreptitiously installed on your computer.
- Whenever possible, try to carry all sensitive files on a portable flash drive. It should be something that can easily be carried discreetly on your person (on a lanyard under your shirt or blouse, for example). That way, even if you are separated from your laptop, your sensitive files can be easily wiped or destroyed. This also frees you from having to obsess over where your laptop is every minute of your trip.
- Both the flash drive and computer should be encrypted, and password protected.

- Free encrypting software is readily available and is often strong enough to prevent hostile access even to most nation state level intelligence services within a reasonable amount of time. (http://www.truecrypt.org). *Under no circumstance, should you share private encryption keys.*
- Never leave a laptop, PDA or important documents in a hotel room unattended because the devices could be stolen, cloned or copied
- If government officials cannot access your data due to strong security encryptions, your computer may be smashed or confiscated out of frustration. This is simply another reason to keep the data on an encrypted flash drive, securely on your person.

Communications

- Internet transmissions like email, instant messaging and video conferencing services such as Skype are easily compromised. As such, exercise due caution when using such communications, or consider the use of an asymmetrically encrypted Internet relay chat (IRC) or email services such as GnuPG for secured communications over the Internet (in addition to VPNs and other forms of encryption).
- Proxy servers such as Tor can be used for more secure Internet browsing.

Personal ID

- In addition to suggestions put forth in Chapter 6, be aware that current US passports and many credit cards have an RFID (radio frequency identification) chip embedded in them, these can be readily scanned even by people on the street. Consider using an RFID shield for your passport/wallet. These are relatively inexpensive and easily purchased.

Cell Phones

Almost all cell phones—even so-called smartphones—are extremely vulnerable to hacking and spyware. Eavesdropping programs that turn the phone into a radio transmitter are readily available and actively in use around the world. They can compromise your phone with nothing more than a simple text message.

Once embedded, spyware of this kind can be used to eavesdrop on conversations within microphone range of the phone—even when the phone is powered off or in airport mode!

There are no effective protections against this type of intrusion, and they are typically undetectable without a thorough system diagnosis by a professional.

The best solution is to remove the battery from the phone completely if you are going into a sensitive meeting or conversation. In the case of phones that don't have a removable battery (such as the iPhone), your best plan is to leave the phone outside the meeting room. This is an inconvenience to be sure, but a necessary one.

Remember that even the best encryption available is only functional if you use it diligently. It takes only a modest investment of time to learn to use encryption effectively, and even the least "tech-savvy" individuals can master the techniques quickly. Be sure to practice with your software several times in a safe environment before you have to use it overseas.

Chapter Ten
WORST-CASE SCENARIOS

"Only after everything goes wrong do we realize we're on our own. And the bigger the disaster, the longer we will be on our own."

—*Amanda Ripley, The Unthinkable*

In this chapter we will address how you can take control when confronted with critical incidents and worst-case scenarios, from kidnappings and arrests to earthquakes, hurricanes and riots.

Although directed toward "thinking about the unthinkable," the material in this chapter is intended neither to scare you into an excess of caution nor to cause a backlash of denial, but rather to provide you with the tools to live—and go about your business—with confidence.

Avoiding Kidnapping

A recent kidnapping of a high-ranking US oil executive occurred early in the morning hours as he stepped from his vehicle to pick up the morning newspaper at the end of his driveway. According to his wife, he did this every day on his way to work. The kidnappers, obviously aware of his routine through prior surveillance, were waiting in a van at the end of the driveway to grab him.

Similarly, a bank CEO was recently kidnapped at gunpoint as he pulled into his regular parking space during the early morning hours. The investigation revealed that the kidnapper had the executive under surveillance and knew that he parked in the identical space at approximately the same time each morning. The bank executive escaped from his kidnapper; however, the oil executive was treated brutally by his abductors and died during captivity.

The vast majority of kidnappings occur when the victim is departing for, or arriving home from, work. As we noted in Chapter 4, the key factor in preventing such easy exposure is to avoid set routines, and maintain situational awareness, whether going to or from work, playing tennis with a friend or going to church.

It should be noted, however, that even if you scrupulously avoid set routines, if you have to return home and park in your garage for example, the only opportunity to launch an attack may be when you are entering or departing your garage, regardless of the schedule you keep. Be mindful of these "choke points" and increase your awareness when entering or leaving these areas or situations. Take precautionary measures whenever possible to secure these areas if possible, either by restricting close access, or through the use of CCTV cameras as examples.

Remember that the first 90 seconds of a kidnapping attempt represent the best opportunity to escape—however, they also pose the greatest danger to life and limb. (Statistically speaking, you're at the greatest risk during the first moments of a kidnapping and during a rescue attempt.)

Surviving an abduction

- Stay calm. Remember that thoughts of anger, denial, and guilt will compromise your ability to think—ultimately your greatest ally in any crisis. You must immediately accept the reality of what is occurring and begin thinking tactically. At this point, it doesn't matter how you got here, only how you're going to get out.
- Follow instructions. Don't give your abductors cause to hurt you.
- Provide a local phone contact to the kidnappers (a company field office or the home or office of a vendor, a distributor, or another business contact) if one is solicited.
- If the situation progresses past the initial abduction phase (first 24-48 hours), it will most likely settle into a captivity phase.
- Once in captivity, anticipate a return of denial and disorientation, followed by depression, during the early days. You may suffer sleep loss and intestinal disorders as well. These symptoms will recede if you are able to reduce stress and adapt to captivity.

- ❖ In 1987, Terry Waite, a peace activist, was abducted by the Islamic Jihad Organization while attempting to negotiate the release of several hostages held in Lebanon. His captivity lasted 1763 days, the first four years in total solitary confinement

❖ He kept his spirits up throughout his captivity by repeating these three phrases to himself:

1. "No regrets—there might have been something you could have done differently to avoid capture but that's little help now."
2. "No self pity—no matter what your situation, there's always somebody worse off than you."
3. "No over-sentimentality—don't look back and wish you'd spent more time with your family or had longer holidays. Life has been lived, you cannot re-live it."

• Adapt by dealing with your abductors in a respectful but not subservient manner. Try to win their respect and sympathy by developing person-to-person relationships with them. Tell them about your family. Show pictures, if possible.
• Eat, rest and exercise as much as possible.
• If you have a clear opportunity to escape, take it, but be mindful that your abductors might have laid a trap for you. Again, statistically, your best chances lie in a negotiated release.
• If the abduction is financially motivated, odds are you will be released if a ransom is paid.
• If the abduction is religiously motivated, say with Islamic fundamentalists, you must understand that the likely hood of you being released unharmed is much lower. As such you should consider all options for escape and weigh them very carefully.

- Stockholm Syndrome—the victim's progressive identification with his or her captors—is considered by many psychologists to be a legitimate risk for abductees. The notion is that small gestures of kindness by some kidnappers, amidst the hostility and sense of fear and helpless, cause abductees to sympathize with the kidnappers. Consider this a similar game to "good cop—bad cop". Understand it for what it is, and always try to maintain a degree of emotional separation from your captors. These people, even the "nice" ones, are holding you against your will and keeping you from your life and family. Moreover, you may have to take decisive, physical action against them to effect your escape in a worst case scenario.
- In the end, always remember that efforts are being made to secure your safe release, and you are not alone.

Arrests

- If you are arrested abroad for any reason, ask permission to notify the nearest U.S. embassy or consulate. In some countries, your request may not be honored immediately. Be persistent.
- A consular officer cannot arrange for free legal aid or provide bail money for you. They can provide you with names of attorneys who speak your language and help you find adequate legal representation. They can also contact your travel companions or relatives, or intervene if you are receiving discriminatory treatment.

Surviving a critical incident

What Is A Critical Incident?

A critical incident may be defined most simply as a situation in which you find yourself in the wrong place at the wrong time—be it a school shooting or a 7.0 Mw earthquake. The scale and cause may be entirely different from one critical incident to another, but the same dynamics tend to apply.

What To Expect In A Critical Incident

In any critical incident, you can expect chaos, and wide spread panic, especially in urban areas. In large-scale critical incidents, such as natural disasters or governmental collapse, you can also expect serious disruptions to communications such as cell phones and internet, transportation gridlock, power outages, food and water supply disruptions, and a breakdown of law enforcement and civil support services.

As we saw with Hurricane Katrina in 2005, the earthquake in Haiti 2010 and the Japan earthquake and "Arab Spring" uprisings of 2011, disaster can strike anywhere with little or no notice.

If a critical incident does occur, you can count on several environmental things to happen very quickly:

- First, mass panic as people attempt to flee the immediate area and civil services attempt to rush in, causing mass confusion.

- Second, massive communications and transportation snarls. Cell phone systems often get overloaded, and depending on the event, avenues of transit and mass transportation systems may either be shut down as a precautionary measure, or simply become impassable due to overwhelming use.

Managing the Chaos

Your priorities in a critical incident—whether as a visitor or as a local—are fundamentally the same.

They are:

1. Get out of the "area of effect" as quickly as possible. (In some cases you may have to evacuate the country altogether.)
2. If you can't get out, be prepared to stay put and "shelter in place" for an extended duration.

Preparedness

In order to be adequately prepared to manage a critical incident, consider the following:

- A primary and secondary plan to get out of the city or country you are staying in, other than air travel if need be (as airports may be closed).
- Keep a emergency preparedness kit or "sac d'évac" (colloquially known simply as a go-bag) handy, whether at home or while traveling (See Appendix B for suggestions).

- Have a communications plan and an "actions-on" plan established with your family and coworkers (i.e., what to do if we get separated, etc.)
- Have coded text messages preplanned to alert family members of your status and actions
- The last thing you want is to try to get to family while they try to get to you through the chaos. Everyone needs to know where to meet up.
- Remember that even when cell lines are jammed, low-bandwidth text communications can oftentimes get through.

The Role of Situational Awareness in Surviving a Critical Incident

Early warning and good intelligence is vital in providing some advanced warning of dangerously unfolding events, and in determining when to execute an evacuation and when to shelter in place.

If you are traveling, advance Warden and STEP intelligence from the U.S. State Department (see Chapter 6) can provide you with the information you need to make good preemptive decisions and avoid being caught unprepared.

If you're attending a large public event, such as a soccer match, or are otherwise in a large crowd, always try to stay on the periphery, the safest place in the event of a panic, stampede, or riot. If a stampede occurs, take shelter behind columns or in doorways or alcoves parallel to the direction of crowd movement.

Ultimately, though you have to exercise good situational awareness as to what's going on around you and decide based upon that data, what's in your best interest—to choose, as they say, "when to hold 'em and when to fold 'em."

In closing . . .

Remember when the unthinkable happens that courage is as contagious as fear. As the Stoic philosophers understood centuries ago, it's not what befalls us that's important but how we choose to respond.

Live With Confidence

Appendix A

DANGEROUS PARCEL INDICATORS

Below are guidelines provided by the US Postal Service for identifying potentially dangerous parcels.

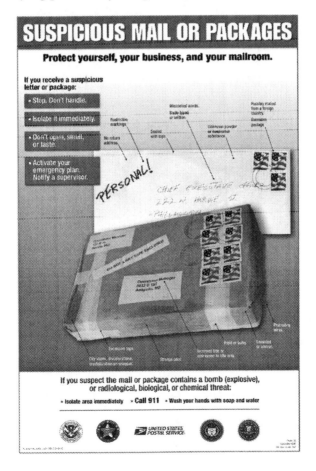

Appendix B

GO-BAG

A *Go-Bag,* or "sac d'évac," is typically a simple backpack or satchel, easily worn or carried. As the first thing you grab in an emergency, it should be adequate to contain the essential tools and provisions to survive a crisis and help you get out of the area of trouble.

Must Haves:

- A good hand-held flashlight (typically a small, bright, tactical light such as law enforcement officers use)
- A portable smoke hood
- Sturdy shoes
- A change of clothes (functional, utility dress such as cargo pants are best)
- A personal (or family) first aid kit
- US and local currency (if international)
- Communications (if traveling internationally, consider a satellite phone)
- Country and/or local area maps
- A supply of any essential medications
- Food and bottled water
- A water purifier

You can survive for an extended period without food, but you *must* have water. In a large-scale disaster, this mean having the ability to purify and drink what water you can find. Be aware that water purifiers are very different than water filters, even though they often look and work similarly. Water purifiers are designed to filter particulates (dirt) and purify water (clear of contaminants). There are many effective, highly portable water purifier systems available commercially. Ensure any you choose are rated for viruses as water sources in many foreign countries are contaminated with viruses.

Dependent on ability and travel circumstances, consider adding the following:

- A utility multi-tool*
- A sturdy field knife*
- Space blanket
- Handheld GPS**
- A good compass**
- Solar-powered recharger for electronics
- Possibly a firearm (if you are trained and permitted to carry one)***

This list is not meant to be all-inclusive, and there are numerous items you might choose to keep in your go-bag not included here. The above are merely meant to provide a guide for essentials to consider traveling with.

* *Traveling internationally with a knife or multi-tool may be problematic due to local laws. Check before you pack.*

** *GPS devises and compasses may be troublesome in some hostile or Muslim countries, as they might be construed as "spy-gear". Use caution when considering traveling with such* *a devise. A stealthy alternative might be to wear a watch with a built in compass. There are numerous digital watches with exceptionally accurate watches on the market.*

**** Possession of a firearm in your Go-Bag would most likely be restricted to your state of residence, and dependent on licensing. INPAX° **does not** recommend firearms for anyone not trained in their use.*

Sam Rosenberg
Founder, INPAX® Academy of Personal Protection
Managing Director, CSI—Corporate Security
& Investigations®

Sam Rosenberg has some two decades of experience in personal protection and security. His Pittsburgh-based company, INPAX, is a leader in private security, defensive tactics, tactical weapons training and critical incident response. Its clients include individuals, corporations, law enforcement agencies and educational institutions nationwide.

Additionally, Mr. Rosenberg is managing director of CSI—Corporate Security & Investigations®, PA Western District, and director of CSI Global Protective Services. CSI provides a full range of investigative and risk management services for a worldwide clientele, including many Fortune 500 companies.

Mr. Rosenberg, a former US Marine Corps officer, has written widely on the management of interpersonal aggression and his views are routinely sought by the news media.

For more information about INPAX or Sam Rosenberg, visit www.LiveWithConfidence.com